In the
Toy Box

My Toys"R"Us Journey Begins

Sal Panicci

ISBN 979-8-88616-301-8 (paperback)
ISBN 979-8-88616-302-5 (digital)

Christian Faith Publishing
832 Park Avenue
Meadville, PA 16335
www.christianfaithpublishing.com

Printed in the United States of America

To all the Toys"R"Us kids, thanks for the memories.

Chapter 1

Major Retailer Seeks Bright, Energetic Individuals

"Try retail. They never lay you off," said a very good friend of mine, whose decisions I respected since he was going to be a millionaire by the time he was thirty-five.

So began my twenty-five years of fun and frolic in service to mankind—and mankind does so want to be serviced. But what did I know? I'm an average person. I thought everyone was like myself. What a boring world it would be if they were, I suppose…

Well, why not then? I said goodbye to the nine-to-five corporate life and hello to "Major Retailer." I was bright, I was energetic (then), and I thought I was individual enough to succeed.

I wrote my cover letter, singing my praises just enough. I made myself sound dependable and yet individual. I listed all my corporate accomplishments. I had a future in the corporate world, but I wanted more. By nature, I wasn't a desk person. I needed to move around.

Three weeks later, and on the same day, I heard two sets of fate-filled words: "We will have your last check ready in two weeks" and "Salvatore? Hi, I'm Joe Cortez. You answered an ad in *The Star-Ledger* for a training program. I'd like you to come in so we can explore your options."

The first sentence was at nine o'clock in the morning, and the other words were uttered at eight o'clock in the evening. That eight o'clock at night should have given me a hint of what was in store—IN STORE. But I had never worked in retail. The truth was, I didn't have a future in the corporate world. I hadn't for the past six months. And now my unemployment was about to run out too.

I made the appointment. I would talk to Joe. It was the appointment that made me the success I am today.

I was a communications major in college, with dreams of working behind the scenes in television. That wasn't to be for lots of reasons. Well, maybe a few reasons. Nah, the one important reason was I just didn't know anyone in the business. Sure, I could have been a DJ in Bismarck, North Dakota—or was that South Dakota?

Anyway, I'm Italian. I was born in New Jersey. I went to school in New Jersey. I still live in New Jersey. I still work in New Jersey. North Dakota or South Dakota, either one was out of the question. Manhattan was like New Jersey. Manhattan was doable. North Dakota? That was the best a suma cum laude graduate from Seton Hall could get?

So I did the unthinkable: I settled. I settled for a career in industrial advertising and for a pattern of being laid off every two to three years. The things we do for money—and for not a lot of money at that. But some money is better than no money. Hopefully, Joe Cortez would change my career path.

On April 23, I reported to a small distribution center in Secaucus, New Jersey. The building wasn't signed. The entrance was difficult to find. When I did pull the doors open, there was a 1960s-style open staircase to be climbed, but at the top was a smiling receptionist. She buzzed Joe Cortez, the human resource manager in charge of recruiting managers for the stores in the New York market.

You could tell he really liked what he did. He interviewed for all management trainees for the stores in New York, New Jersey, Long Island, and parts of Connecticut. If he liked you, the next step was talking to the regional vice president. I was impressed. I was nervous, though. Don't know why. I really didn't want the job, especially when I heard the salary—or lack thereof. It was almost half of what I was making before I was laid off.

I guess my expression gave me away. It was very impressive before he told me what my salary was gonna be. Of course, I got the bull about all the benefits being part of my total compensation. But you can't buy groceries with benefits. You can't pay your car insurance with benefits. What Joe neglected to tell me was that I wouldn't have time to enjoy money, anyway. Retail's not a job. It's a way of life.

Finally, Joe said he could get me a little more money. He thought I would do "well" with the company. He said that I "had what it took." Well, I had heard all that before. It seems that there is stock phrasing for closing an interview.

"I need to discuss your qualifications with the RVP, and I'll let you know the next steps by the end of the week," said Joe.

He stood up. I stood up. We walked the fifty yards to the receptionist, shook hands, and said goodbye.

I expected to get a letter in the mail. It didn't come. No phone call either. The interview was on a Tuesday. The weekend came and went, and still no reach-out from Joe. I didn't want to make less. So why was I disappointed?

I guess any money is better than no money. So coached Mom, and her sageness was reinforced by my creditors. Actually, Mom made it clear that "I wasn't living off her" for the rest of my life. My mom loved me, but Tina gave tough love. When she kicked you in the ass, it was for a reason. And she was always right. She worked hard to raise three kids on her own. I was grown now. I was living at home because I had no choice, but if I lived there, I had to contribute.

With no money coming in, my contribution to the household dried up. This was not a good thing in Mom's eyes, and I understood. But Mom knew me. I was getting depressed, and the more depressed I became, the less energy I put into searching for work. Mom's philosophy was that any job was a good job as long as it was a job.

Growing up, I never worked in retail after school, and I never waited tables. Everyone should try both in their youth. You really learn a lot about human nature. I needed money. The New Jersey Meadowlands needed waiters—"no experience needed." I was perfect for the job. It was soccer season. If I didn't need the money, it truly would have been fun. I made a whopping $50 that weekend. Tina got half. That was okay because that Monday at dinnertime, Joe called. He offered me the position of management trainee—starting immediately.

Mom was happy. Joe was happy. I was…well, I wasn't unhappy.

So back to Secaucus I went. I met the regional vice president. I met several of the other trainees. I met the district manager for the stores I would train at. I met…I met…I met… I got my schedule. I started tomorrow. "Tomorrow there would be sun." But that's retail. Decisions are slow in coming, but once the decision is made, it's time to jump through hoops to make it happen.

So bright and early on Monday morning (it was actually 9:00 a.m.), I found myself in Livingston, New Jersey.

I knocked and knocked, but no one would let me in. Finally, a woman with very dark, very long hair; very red lips; and very high heels answered my exit-door knock. That's right; employees (*associates* in today's world) entered the store through the exit door if the store was still closed. This wasn't gonna be so bad. Then she said hello and shook my hand. Did I say she had very long nails?

Toni (as she liked to be called) had so much energy. She was hard to keep up with. She told me to stay at the front of the store. When Toni directed, you obeyed. Employee after employee strolled in—happy, laughing, not afraid at all. I truly envied them. I soon learned that it wasn't the job that made them happy. It was all the after-work personal activities the employees looked forward to.

Finally, another trainee strolled in. It was Dan. He introduced himself to me, thinking I was a member of management in the store. It was my first half hour on the job, and already, I carried myself like a member of management. I guess I was a fast learner.

Dan and I would become hard-and-fast friends all through the training program. We traveled in the same rotation. We became the team of Dan and Sal. What a team we were. He did the right side of the gym set for display, and I did the left. His side faced in, and mine faced out. One of us had to be wrong, and it was usually Dan. When we put bikes together, yep, he had more parts left over than me. When we did the weekly price changes, after I found all my items, we started looking for his.

But he could unload a truck in an hour when it took most employees three. He could make even the most everyday chore an experience in fun, and he had all the employees eating out of his hand. I guess he was definitely management material too. Joe Cortez really knew his business.

So did Toni. She could direct a store with the best of them, and she would never break a nail—a definite feat for a merchandise manager. The merch manager had the responsibility of the selling floor. The operations manager ran the front of the store. Since a store exists for selling, someone who can get everything out onto the sales floor so it could be sold is a treasure.

Toni was a treasure, but Livingston was a rusty old treasure chest. It was a hard store to run. There was no employee workforce from the community since it was a fairly wealthy area, so employees came from the Newark area. This was a real hike for the salary that was being offered. However, there was a local contingent of colorful, hardworking Filipinos on the job in this store, and they did a great job regardless of the language barrier. In fact, the one thing I still remember was the daytime maintenance man cleaning the bathrooms and the floors and leaving the scent of orange when done. I guess he was twenty years ahead of his time.

Dan and I arrived just in time to help with the summer seasonal phase changes. We were the mules. Fixtures needed to be moved from the front to the rear of the store, and then these fixtures needed to be cleaned and merchandised. Easy. A piece of cake. Yeah, right. Each fixture came with its own blueprint of what items needed to go where. The challenge was finding these items in the storeroom.

Just like my own closet, nothing was ever where it should be. But my closet wasn't twenty thousand square feet. So Dan and I took turns looking and seeking. It was more like hide-and-seek. But we were a good team, and Toni was a good merchandising teacher. But I really wasn't a fan of the Toni method. Rather than showing what was being done wrong during the course of the project, she'd critique the finished product, and it basically had to be done all over again.

But the hard part was done. The product was there. It was just a matter of tightening and striping and shoeboxing a different way. In hindsight, I guess it stuck with you better if you had to repeat the entire exercise. For our team, the third time was the charm. By day 3, Dan and I were experts, so it was time for our own responsibilities.

They broke up the team. Dan stayed on the selling floor. I went to the front of the store and worked with the cashiers and the safe and the money and the customer issues and Billy, the operations manager.

Billy was a great guy. He kind of resembled Santa. He had gray hair, very white skin, and rosy cheeks and nose. But Billy had one personal issue: he was somewhat odoriferous. I don't know if the problem existed with his clothing or his person, but you couldn't be too near to Billy for any length of time. In retail, this has its good points and bad. He seldom dealt with customer issues since they would walk away from him sooner than they needed. This was good for Billy but bad for other managers since we needed to finish the assist and answer the question that was always asked: "When was the last time he bathed?"

But Billy knew his job even though he wanted the sales floor. If he knew he could trust his assistant, then he would be out on the sales floor merchandising and trying to help guests. Which meant that Toni could do other things, like actually visit other stores in the neighborhood to see what was going on or take a long lunch. In retail, you learn to seize the moment and take advantage of every free minute you get since there will be even more times when the moments take advantage of you and you leave the store two or three hours later than scheduled.

So those who worked the front end of the store learned their job quickly. Your only other alternative was having Billy sitting next to you for eight to nine hours. No one wanted that. The purpose of the training program was to develop strengths. Dan was developing strong arms. I was developing intestinal fortitude. Who knew you needed a strong stomach to work in retail?

The front-end responsibilities could be broken down into three functions: money, guest services, and security pickups. The first order of the day was to run opening reports and put the cash drawers out in all the registers. Opening took about half an hour, so you definitely had to be at the store at 9:00 a.m. if the store opened at 9:30 a.m. Tills were numbered by register numbers, so you had to be careful to place the right till in the right register. You also needed to ensure the security of the safe when you were putting the drawers out, meaning you needed keys and combinations you were not supposed to have as a trainee but you did because you needed them to function.

Once the registers were set, you needed to make your cashier schedule based on who showed up for work.

Usually, at least one cashier called in sick. Usually, your head cashier did the daily cash report from the previous day, but since I was a trainee, this was my responsibility. This was an electronic report that had to match up to what the register said it did. If you were $1 off, you were fine. If you were more than $1 off, you had to find where the discrepancies were and all by 11:00 a.m. since the area office needed to know your sales figure by that time so the company profitability could be published.

Every day, I was searching. I searched the trash. I searched the cash drawers since charge slips and cash could slip behind the drawer. I reconciled the type of transactions. I counted the safe. To this day, my own checkbook doesn't balance to the dollar. For me, this was a difficult chore. I never liked dealing with money, but I learned to treat it like a game. Sometimes I won, and sometimes I lost. But the playing of the game was always fun, especially since I knew Billy could always isolate the issue if I couldn't. After all, it was his responsibility. Thank God he would tell you to go to the service area to help out when he hunted!

Balancing required each register to be at $100 in cash, plus the scheduled cash on hand in the safe. Billy always found a way to balance. But of course, he couldn't show me how. I had to find out myself when I became an ops manager. The trick was, you always needed to have an extra $20 on you. And the next day, when you were $20 over, you would take it back and be balanced again. No store wanted issues with the store safe.

But as a trainee, you did your best to make things balance before you called Billy. You felt responsible, and you didn't want to go to Guest Services too quickly because that meant you had to deal with people! At least that's what they used to be before they came into the store, and I suppose that is what they turned back into when they left the store. But when they were at the Guest Services counter, they were in defense mode.

You could see it in their eyes. They threw you the return and expected to hold you at the ten-yard line so it was easier for them to score. And score they did because the guest was always right—that is, if the store managers said they were. We had such a liberal return policy at this time, anyway. If you could push it, drag it, or carry it in, we would take it back regardless of its condition. It could be three years old and outgrown by the child, and if the guest had the cojones to take it to the store for a refund (dirty and/or broken), we took it back. They got it as a gift, of course, and their child played with it for only a week before this secondhand three-year-old item broke. But we took it back. The bike could have a ripped seat and rusty wheels, and we took it back. The coat could have food stains and ring around the collar, and we took it back. We took back anything, it seemed, except when the guest "insisted" we take it back. Usually, this was when the manager was called to the service area, and if the guest was really insistent, Billy was paged to deal with the guest directly. We were the only store with Billy—secret weapon number 5.

Two other functions of Guest Services were to ensure no paying guest waited in line and that the pickup booth at the front of the store for electronic items was always staffed. Register lines were not to exceed three guests, and if they did, the last guest on the line would call out or snap their fingers and expect another register to open. And of course, the electronics pickup booth could have its employee on duty and no one needed a pickup. As soon as this employee went on break, it seemed as if every guest in the store needed to pick up their item at the booth. And since most of these people waited in line at the registers already, they were sure tapping their toes and fuming while waiting in another line to pick up the items they had already paid for.

But the worst situation was the guest who had to be at school to pick up their child in five minutes but wanted to make a return without a receipt, knowing the item was bought at Kmart since it did have the Kmart price label still on it. They didn't have the time to fill out the return slip. They didn't have the time for you to look up the item number, and they certainly didn't have the time to argue over the amount of their refund. The price sticker on the item may have stated $9.99, but since we were selling it for $11.99, they insisted they be refunded the $11.99 retail.

Fifteen minutes later, they took the $9.99 and left in a huff since it was our fault their child would be waiting outside school in the cold and unsupervised. And the final last words uttered by this guest as she stormed out the store usually were "What's your name? I'm going to complain to your office." I soon learned to say my name was, of course, Billy.

Chapter 2

The World Revolves around Season

Well, training would take Dan and me to Nanuet, New York; to Paramus, New Jersey; and finally to Totowa, New Jersey. Totowa is an American Indian name, and HOW appropriate it was to refer to this store by the city name since, in this case, it felt as if the guests were always on the warpath. I spent my first "season" in Totowa, New Jersey, right around the corner from my home—well, almost. But close didn't mean easy. Although looking back, I think Totowa was the most fun of my retail career.

The last leg of my training was in Totowa. The day Dan and I began at the Totowa store, we met the DM (director of merchandising) for this store for the first, but not the last, time. His name was Scott. He was a big burly guy with a thick Western European accent. In his younger years, he played professional ice hockey in Chicago. Upon being injured, he joined the retail workforce and worked his way up to DM in the New Jersey market.

Scott was a very deliberately demonstrative guy—always the instructor and always making sure that you knew the reasoning behind the task at hand. If you listened, you did appreciate the knowledge and the amount of pride he took in his job. I always listened. I always appreciated his help and input. And I always appreciated the man. He was always a gentleman with me even after our shaky first meeting.

It was 5:30 p.m.—time for Dan and me to punch out. I got to the breakroom first where there was about to be an employee meeting that Scott requested. I happened to be at the time clock when the meeting began. I punched my card, and Dan motioned to me to punch him out as well since he would have had to make his way through the crowd to the other side of the room. Upon doing so, this big hand attached to this really big arm grabbed my wrist and pulled me, almost dragging me, to the back of the room. This big arm and hand were attached to, yep, Scott.

He introduced himself to me in his very-thought-out, very-instructional method of speech. He asked who I was and where I worked in the store. I introduced myself and acknowledged that I was a trainee and, as such, I still had a lot to learn since he proceeded to tell me that what I did could be considered fraud. Under no circumstance is anyone permitted to punch another employee's time card.

"Doesn't this make sense?" he asked. Then he continued, "If we permitted punching of others' time cards, then anyone can be adding hours on to a buddy's time card without that buddy actually working."

It made perfect sense. Anything would have made perfect sense coming from a wrestler-looking guy who caught me in the act of doing something wrong.

He told me not to ever do it again, and he motioned for Dan to come over as well, and Dan got the same speech. So what was initially an effort not to disrupt the meeting had everyone kind of keeping one eye on Scott and one eye on Glen, the store director who was leading the meeting. But even though one eye was on Glen, all ears were on Scott. It was as if E. F. Hutton were speaking. But Scott loved the role of teacher. This situation was right up his alley, and he made sure it was an example that the entire store should learn from since no employee should ever punch in or out another employee's time card.

After twenty minutes, Dan and I were permitted to leave. We learned two things in that twenty minutes—well, actually, *three* things:

Punching someone else's time card is grounds for termination.

Shortcuts never really end up being shortcuts.

You always had to make nice with your store's DM.

Dan and I both had it easy with points 1 and 2, but Dan would not find number 3 as understandable and comfortable. It seems Scott either liked you or not. I was lucky. He liked me and my work ethic.

Dan was not so lucky. If Dan felt something was wrong, he was gonna make sure everyone involved knew how he felt. He couldn't let the little meaningless events of the day go without imparting his wisdom. And this was surprising since Dan was basically a quiet, get-the-job-done type of guy.

Scott liked his authority, and he knew how to use it. Every associate in the store knew who he was, and each went out of his or her way to shine in front of him 'cause if he liked you, you had it much easier than if he didn't. But it wasn't an ego trip with Scott. He wanted to do well with and for the company, and he wanted everyone under him to excel also. He liked getting in the thick of things, getting his hands dirty. And he liked to instruct. He especially liked to instruct Dan for the conflict and me for my quickness and attention to detail. Only kidding! He liked teaching me because he would show me how he would do it, and I would become a little Scott, his mini-me, and do it exactly as he wanted it done. Not that there was a right or wrong in lots of instances. Scott just liked things done his way, and his way was not Dan's way in many instances.

The morning after the time card episode, when Dan and I showed up at the store, Glen pulled us aside and asked about our experience with Scott. He told us that after the associate meeting, Scott remarked to him that he thought Dan and I would do well. So we had to. Scott was never wrong.

Actually, Glen and Scott liked to challenge each other. As the weeks flew by, we would discover that they were both cut from the same cloth. They were peas in the same pod. They were both captains on the same ship. They were both charming ladies' men, each in his own way. They were both big guys—guys other guys enjoyed drinking with after hours. They were both with the company for about ten years, and both had the love and respect of their employees. This was important since salaries at the store level were certainly not a source for motivation. It was so difficult to hire and then keep good workers. A good cashier or a good sales floor person was really worth their weight in gold, and they were constantly nickeled-and-dimed. But this was our life in the toy box. If your staff liked you, you got lots accomplished. If you were mean or belittling, you got sabotaged.

Reshop is an important skill to learn. One of the managers at the Totowa store, Donna, was very skilled at teaching the proper method of reshop. Toward the end of each shift, any returned merchandise collected at the customer service area or from the registers needed to be placed back on the shelves so it could be resold. Sometimes finding the correct location on the sales floor for this merchandise was difficult, especially if you did not deal with that merchandise on a regular basis. If Donna was on duty, she would walk through the area and drop on the floor any piece of merchandise that was placed in the wrong location. She seemed to relish in this method. And since employees and trainees could not clock out till your shopping cart of reshop was completely empty, she did not win any popularity contests even if she was right. All product did need to be on the sales floor where it belonged. She just didn't have to openly enjoy the process so much.

Well, training finally came to an end, and Dan and I were given our assignments for season. We both passed. We were both assistant managers now. That trainee label came off. But we would find that training never really ended, especially when you worked with the public. But Dan would spend season in Nanuet, New York, and I would remain in Totowa. Nanuet wasn't a Scott store. And since I did things Scott's way, I was assigned to Totowa. I worked well under pressure. Actually, I worked till the job was done, and in Scott's eyes, that was the same thing.

Glen gave me the boys' toys and sporting goods to handle. All in all, I had five aisles to manage. Through the end of September, I worked by myself, and I kept my aisles spick-and-span. My store-room shelves were also easy to find things on. But when October hit, I felt like I went to hell. Between the re-shop every day and the dou-ble the number of trucks the store received each day and the constant customer questions, I couldn't keep up. But I couldn't be the first guy fired from retail! No one is ever fired from retail.

Finally, Glen gave me help. I had my own worker: Jerry. He was in the first wave of seasonal new hires.

He was strong. He was bright. He was full-time. He was everything a sales floor associate should be. What he wasn't was in my section. I constantly had to seek him out. He liked to socialize—LOTS. Well, I wasn't gonna put up with that. I constantly complained to Glen. He consistently said he would speak with him, but I always had to go looking. Finally, I had to have my own understanding with Jerry. I would outline what needed to be done that day and give him only specific tasks that he did finish by his shift's end.

I was annoyed with Glen and with Scott for making me put up with Jerry's socializing, but it seemed that he was in their social circle as well. I was doomed.

But as we got closer to November, I did get two evening employees who were wonderful: Sussie and Tony. Sussie was a grammar school teacher just working for some extra holiday cash. Tony was a construction worker with five kids. He was definitely working to get out of the house for a while. But we had fun. When I worked the late shift, they were always doing what they needed to do. When I worked the early shift, I would wait for them to come in before I left the store to tell them what needed to be done. They'd listen intently, then they would laugh and tell me what they would do for me. It was a good compromise.

There was no compromising with Jerry. Even Tony and Sussie would get pissed at Jerry during the hour that their shifts overlapped. This made me feel good since I then knew that there was definitely something going on with Jerry. Actually, because of Jerry, Sussie and Tony worked even harder. They didn't want to see me get in trouble. I was really flattered. Sussie and Tony were my reason for going to work, and when I resigned myself to the fact that Jerry was a lazy slacker who could only accomplish a limited number of tasks during the course of the day, my days did improve.

I especially liked the big-truck aisle. It was easy to restock since the items were big and stacked well. So that was my aisle. Jerry ended up doing what he could in Sporting Goods. Scott constantly reprimanded me for the condition of the Sporting Goods aisle. Since Jerry was his pal (I think I was a little jealous of that too), what could I do or say? I just agreed with him and tried to make it better even though *better* did not exist in a teacher's vocabulary. Either it was the way Scott liked it or it was bad.

All through training, I kept seeing these ugly dolls being returned at the service area. It seems that they came with a birth certificate and a form to change their name. I don't know why or how they were plentiful during the summer, but when September hit, stores couldn't get enough of them. The Cabbage Patch Kids craze had begun. And when they were plentiful, you would think that my family members would have bought them. Of course not! They had to wait till everybody else in the world needed them for them to need them too. And since I worked in the toy box, they couldn't understand why I wasn't able to get one or two for their friends as well.

I was only an assistant manager. Glen would help me out when he could, but we had waiting lists. So I would put relatives and friends of relatives on the waiting list and sneak their slips earlier in the pile so they would at least have theirs in time for Christmas.

When the craze first began, we merchandised them like we normally would. There was a doll section at the front of the store, and eight feet of this area was supposed to be filled with Cabbage Patch dolls—that is, Kids. The store would ensure that this section was filled before the doors were unlocked for business each morning. This procedure was followed for a month, and the Kids (Cabbage Patch Kids, not *dolls*) would sell out by the end of each day.

It was 9:00 a.m. on October 8, and it was time to unlock the doors. It was like a stampede of buffalo. Our first line of determined moms had formed prior to the store opening unbeknownst to the store staff. Once the doors opened, the human animal was unleashed. The pulling, the screaming, the crying—and that was just the store staff (only kidding). The store staff remained with their mouths dropped open.

When the dust settled, there was one lonely box in the center of the gondola. A gondola in retail lingo is not a boat but the shelving fixture. A middle-aged man in his Brooks Brothers suit made the perfect swan dive over the moms arguing three feet deep in the aisle. He landed stomach first on the top shelf of the gondola. He grabbed that last Cabbage Patch Kid, stood up as if he were not the Olympian we all thought him to be, and confidently walked to the first open register to check out. I swear he had to be hurt. He had dented the shelving.

This was my first experience with the "Gotta have" parent syndrome. Their child wants this toy and therefore will have this toy at all costs!

The arguing moms finally went on their way but not until they found out when the next shipment would be in. No one in the store really knew. At that point, our trucks were not manifested. The only way we knew what was on a truck was when the truck was unloaded. But they would be back at the store at the arrival of *any* truck pulling into the truck bay. I swear they had a lookout on our roof. No sooner would the truck arrive than the mom line would start to build. "Are they here yet?" was the question of every day. And they would camp out like how they would to get the best seats at the concert of their dreams. It was amazing.

Eventually, the mom Cabbage Patch routine would be as follows:

1.   Put your name and phone number on the waiting list.
2.   Find out when the next truck was arriving at the store.
3.   If it was 3:00 p.m. and the truck was unloaded already, stay in line since the store would probably get another truck before closing.
4.   If the store did get another truck before closing, plead with the store manager to peek inside to see if there were any Cabbage Patch Kids on the truck.
5.   If you got a manager who was foolish enough to look, convince him or her to unload the truck.

Yes, we had a waiting list, but at this time legally we needed to sell some to the general public every day as well. So at least some of these determined moms or moms-in-the-know would always end up with a Kid (doll).

As Christmas approached, special dignitaries needed and received Cabbage Patch Kids too. Rank brings with it privilege. After all, their kids and grandkids also needed to have the popular item of the season. So the double bagging in the office began, and the parking lot fights and parking lot sales began also. Just because someone was able to get one didn't mean they had to keep it when they could sell it for $250!

But as with life in general, in the midst of the bad, if you really look hard, you'll find some good. With me, that good came in the form of a mom-to-be. She stumbled into the Totowa store after visiting other locations. She said she watched the store employees as they dealt with the public. She singled me out. She could tell I was a pushover. But she phrased it much more politely. She said I "really conducted myself in a humane, compassionate manner." I wasn't "short." Oh boy! I was in for it. But since I understood "short" not to mean in stature but temperament, she had my attention.

Her story in this *Naked City* of Cabbage Patch experiences was simple. She was to be a mom for the first time right before Christmas. She was having twins—yes, she was! She was having a boy and a girl. She needed a boy kid and a girl kid with pigtails. Hair color didn't matter. Didn't need to have a pacifier or a twinkle in the eye. She would officially change the names, or maybe she would name her kids the names of the Cabbage Patch Kids she was hoping to get if she liked their names.

This was her story, and she was hoping I could get her two. She knew of the special dispensations. Her neighbor was the wife of a local dignitary and told her she had gotten two for her kids. She stopped talking and waited. I didn't know what to say. It wasn't my store. I was only an assistant manager and at Glen's mercy. I took her phone number and said I would investigate and call her. She believed me. I believed me.

Well, it was almost time to go home. I would close the next day. As the night shift came in, most of the managers were going home. It would be me on the sales floor and Ed up front and a trusted employee on the back door. Since I really was spread thin, I took my name tag off. I didn't have time to deal with the moms waiting in line. I totally avoided that aisle. It seemed that everyone working was doing a good job, and the Cabbage Patch waiting-list people who were called in the morning were starting to come in to get their Kids.

We had the Kids set up on display in the storeroom, out of view of the public. Anyone called would be given a sales slip that they needed to pay for and would then be instructed to come to the back entrance to the storeroom to pick up a Kid. The light bulb went off. I called my mom-to-be. Five minutes after hanging up, she was at the store. She sought me out, and I gave her two tickets. She chose two kids with great names, and I could still see her tears of joy as she left the store.

I felt good. Deceptive but good. Plus I felt empowered. Wow, was this how it felt to be a manager? No wonder Glen walked around constantly puffed up. It could be a real trip.

Well, the empowerment didn't last too long. The next day, Scott again let me know how bad Sporting Goods looked. Glen was spouting all over the store. Jerry was at his social best. Suddenly, the feeling from last night was just a memory. One to be forgotten.

It was a very busy Saturday, the last Saturday before Christmas. At two o'clock in the afternoon, I heard my name paged. I walked up to the service area, and there I shook hands with a man carrying a shopping bag. He introduced himself as the husband of the lady who was having twins. I could feel the corners of my mouth rising. I was smiling. I said it was nice to meet him. He informed me that the twins arrived last week. Mom and babies Kelsey and Sal were doing just fine. I felt so flattered and so good.

I congratulated him and thanked him for letting me know. As I turned to walk away, he grabbed my arm. He said his wife made him come to the store to deliver this gift for my kindness, and he would not allow me to refuse this gift. (We weren't allowed to accept gifts.) He shook my hand again and walked out of the store and my life.

I brought the bag to the manager's office and took it home that night. I never heard from either of them again. I would have made a good godfather. Oh well. But every year, when I bring out the three-foot ceramic-class-made Christmas tree and plug it in, I feel really warm and wonder what those two kids are doing today. Kelsey and Sal. They're now in their late teens. I know they had a good childhood. I just know.

Well, Christmas Eve finally came. The store closed at 8:00 p.m., and I was shocked at how many last-minute shoppers there really are. It was a very busy day. Of course, we couldn't leave at 8:00 p.m. We had to get the store ready for returns on the day after Christmas. Register counters needed to be turned around, and an area needed to be stanchioned off for the expected lines to form. Then there was the champagne that needed to be toasted. It was very nice of Glen to have champagne for the managers.

Glen toasted to a great season. His store—our store—was up 20 percent over the previous year. A great season indeed. If it were to be a great inventory, we would all get bonuses. After several toasts, Glen turned to me and toasted my patience and my ability to still get the job done in spite of Jerry, our store's undercover security.

I remained with my mouth hanging open. I should have been mad, but I wasn't. I was tired and just wanted to get home to enjoy the remainder of Christmas Eve at my brother's. Undercover—I felt like I was in a bad movie.

It truly is amazing how quickly Christmas came and went. I felt like I had no time off whatsoever.

Since I was new, my job for the day after Christmas was to be on register giving refunds. Receipts or no receipts, opened and unopened, our items and those from other retailers—I saw them all. Okay, so we sold the same things as other retailers, but why should we have to take back something bought somewhere else? Glen made it clear that this was "our policy," so I took everything back as instructed.

For the first two weeks after Christmas, every day found our store in the red. We refunded more dollars than items being purchased. We went from $100,000 sale days to negative $25,000 days. And even though it seems that everyone but me knew of our liberal return policy ahead of time, it was *Naked City* time again with thousands of stories. It was fun watching and listening.

To this day, I am still a novice on return stories. Even when I tell the truth, the clerk has the look of disbelief. And why does one need a story when one has the receipt? That little piece of paper is worth more than the biggest of stories any day. But human nature's nature is not to be silent. Like Jerry, it is to be social.

I still can't believe he was part of store security, and supposedly, he caught thieving employees and shoplifters without ever breaking his cover. Wow, I'm glad he never knew about the ceramic Christmas tree—or did he?

Scott never spoke about Jerry to me. I never asked. I had my pride too. Till the day I left the Totowa store, on each visit he would tell me how bad Sporting Goods looked. But after Christmas, he had kind of a twinkle in his eye. I guess I did things Scott's way even when I didn't know.

Two days before inventory, I was told that I was being transferred to the Paramus store. I would start on Monday, the day after Totowa's inventory. Paramus's inventory would be the week after. Lucky me, I got to be part of two inventories. Yes, lucky me! Work is work! Especially in retail, the hours are always there to be worked. But having the respect of your teammates is special.

As soon as the word got out that I was leaving the store, Sussie and Tony started circulating a petition to keep me at Totowa. Apparently, this had never happened before. This was the first time I heard Scott laugh—this deep gutsy laugh. Of course, on my last day in Totowa, I was honored with a cake and parting gifts—a good laugh from Scott, a handshake from Glen, a sterling pen-and-pencil set from the associates at Tony and Sussie's insistence.

But the best gift of all was getting to know and work with Sussie and Tony: two very special people. I never saw them again. The petition was placed in my file.

Chapter 3

Paramus: A Small Store, a Big Challenge

So with a heavy heart, I arrived at the Paramus store at 9:00 a.m. on Monday. The same management team was there as when I trained. The manager of the store was already at work since this store was always wrecked from the weekend sales. The saving grace of the Paramus store was that it was closed on Sundays due to Bergen County, New Jersey, blue laws. So regardless of the state of the store (what was done or still needed to be done), at midnight on Saturday, the store needed to be locked. The city felt so strongly about these rules that the police were waiting outside the store at 11:20 p.m. each Saturday to enforce the closure.

It was a great perk from the worker perspective, especially during the Christmas holidays when employee store cleanup abuses really became the norm. But in Paramus on Saturday, everyone knew they'd be out of the store at midnight, not two o'clock or three o'clock in the morning. And if you were the manager scheduled to have Monday off, it worked out great. I, along with the merchandising manager, would be the one enjoying the Sundays and Mondays off.

As usual, the operations manager wanted to be more of a merchandising manager, and the merchandising manager wanted nothing to do with front-end operations. Joe was the merchandising manager, and Al was the operations manager. Both were excellent at their jobs, but everyone knew there was a rivalry going on in the store between the two managers.

This store was smaller than Totowa in size, but because of its easy access from New York City, it was usually higher in traffic and sales than Totowa, even with it being closed on Sunday. So there was no time for the simple amenities. It was a "This is what needs to be done, and just get it done" situation. Joe shook my hand, gave me a two-page list of tasks to be done for the day, and basically went on his way.

The store employees remembered me from my training days, and I remembered the layout of the store. In reality, there was no issue with this approach, but personally, I went from being really special in the eyes of the employees in Totowa to just another assistant manager in Paramus. Fame is truly fleeting, and you really are only as good as your last picture. I guess I would have to create another award-winning picture for Paramus.

But Joe was no Mr. DeMille. I had to show Joe he could depend on me, so I got down to task number 1. I was put in charge of the video game and electronics aisle. It wasn't the time of Nintendo and Sega but rather of Commodore 64 and Atari. These sections required a lot of product displays that consisted of actual products mounted on pegboards that hung from an overhead metal pipe. These sections could hold up to sixty or more displays based on the item being in stock.

There were no displays up in these aisles when I arrived. Without displays, these products could not be sold. These items were not placed on the sales floor due to theft and pilferage issues. These displays were used to dispense purchase tickets so customers could purchase them. Theoretically, each display should have had one ticket for each item in stock. The customer needed to pull off one of these tickets in order to buy the item. This ticket was rung at the register. Without displays, nothing was being sold in these sections. And this was only one of twenty-four tasks that needed to get done this Monday. But I did have Sally to help me.

First thing we needed to do was take an inventory of the security storeroom and bring out one of each item so the displays could be created. Once the display was created, the pull tickets needed to be handwritten and attached to each display based on the inventory we counted. And it was just me and Sally. Not Sally and I. Definitely me and Sally against the world.

It took all day just to get task number 1 accomplished! Joe wasn't happy.

I too was upset, but Sally took it in stride. Apparently, this was the order of business every Monday. Since the store is so busy on Saturday, even the floor samples sell. If there were no tickets hanging from the display, the guest was asked if they wanted to buy the floor model. There was not enough time for the section manager to walk to the storeroom to check the inventory levels. It was easier to tell the customer that this was the last item. The box was part of the display, so the customer was happy to buy the floor sample (even at no discount). But due to this approach, the store became void of all the displays necessary to sell from.

We couldn't allow this to happen every week. It was too much work to replace them, and there were too many lost sales involved. Since my iron day was Saturday, I would be the one to prevent this from happening again. Or so I thought.

Now, in retail, an "iron day" was the day one worked from opening to closing. That meant being in the store from 9:30 a.m. to 9:30 p.m. with an extra hour and a half after closing to help pull the store back together again.

Years later, when I had the opportunity to travel to other parts of our wonderful country to visit our stores, it was perfectly clear that the customers in the New York metropolitan area are a breed of their own. Only here do moms walk in to return ten or more items with only five minutes to devote to the process. Only here would someone open a factory-sealed box to ensure it had all its pieces and then discard it on the floor for another sealed box from the shelf. Why not take the one they knew had all the pieces to the register? What was the purpose of opening the box? Only here would a customer waiting in line snap their fingers and tell the manager to open another register. And only here would a manager take these orders from the customer and open another register. And only in the New York metro area (Brooklyn in particular) could you tell a customer to go f——ck himself or herself and get away with it. However, the rule was, the customer needed to bestow those words upon management first, and then management could reply.

But it was Sally and me against the world of the gaming kids and the gaming kids' parents who had not a clue as to what their kids were looking for but couldn't leave the store without it. Sally worked till 5:00 p.m. on Saturday and was off on Monday as well. There was no one in our section on Monday since it was our slowest day, and the rest of the store needed to be stocked and straightened. This week, I would be working six days. But today was Monday, the slowest day!

The biggest problem with our section was that it was en route to all the other sections of the store. So Sally was the number 1 answer lady, and she did it well since she did like to socialize. The more socializing, the less work was done in my section. Sally would need to learn how to tolerate me since I was constantly looking for her as she toured with the customers through the store. But on the bright side, she had the fastest hand in the east. She could write tickets faster than anyone I had ever seen. I needed to harness this talent, but Sally didn't want to be harnessed.

Working in retail, you discover very quickly that everyone has his or her own special scent. Nail biters smell like dried saliva. Heavy smokers smell like ashtrays. Heavy smokers who use perfume or cologne smell like a lightly used ashtray. There was one cashier who smelled like lilies of the valley. One of the other sales floor employees smelled like Jack Daniels. A few other employees just smelled. Sally, on the other hand, didn't smell. You could tell she had a tough upbringing, but she was very civil to me. And she knew her job. My challenge was keeping her nose to the grindstone so that she did her job.

For a couple of weeks, she felt me out. She liked that I wasn't above assisting her, and we both laughed about some of the really stupid rules we had to deal with. For instance, our store prided itself on always being in stock. If an item was temporarily out of stock, the display needed to be taken off the floor. We weren't allowed to just stick a Temporarily Out of Stock notice on the item.

The larger displays hanging from the overhead pipe were no problem. The problems arose with the software displays. These games were alphabetized by game type. Taking one game out in the middle of the display meant that all the other games following it needed to be moved also to close up the space that was created by the removal of this one game. The real aggravation was that as soon as the display was removed, a truck arrived delivering this item, so the space now had to be opened up to once again include this item in the display. Hours of wasted time.

But this was our job. Sally laughed. Till the day I left that store, every time I adjusted displays due to out-of-stock situations or I saw Sally doing it, I verbalized a little too loudly how stupid this process was. This would always make the corners of Sally's mouth rise even when she wasn't speaking to me, which seemed to increase as the months flew by.

And as the months passed, Sally went from not particularly having a scent of her own to constantly smelling like this sickeningly sweet lilac fragrance. It was due to the gum she would chew. But as much as I upset her, I also made her laugh. She had pains in her stomach after laughing at me fall off the overstock at the front of the store because I leaned back too far to try to grab the video game system she was handing me. I fell ten feet, and Sally laughed.

Then there was the time we had to hang this heavy plastic manufacturer logo sign from a display pipe that was attached to the shelving fixture in our aisle, Sally on one side and me on the other. We got it hooked on the pipe. The heavy lifting made Sally have to go to the ladies' room. As she left, I put her ladder away. When I came back to the aisle to put my ladder away, I noticed the sign was listing to the right and the fixture bracket was quickly bending due to the weight of the sign. Since the ladies' room was near the break room, Sally decided to also take her break. So there I hung for fifteen minutes as the counterbalance till she came back from her break.

Not one customer had time to get another manager to help me no matter how politely I asked. They saw me hanging off the pipe, but it was lunchtime, and they had to get what they needed and get out. A few of the older ladies who passed even asked me where they could find the items they were looking for in the same tone as if I were standing on the floor next to them. I calmly gave them directions. It was too surreal. Here I was doing chin-ups. I would think I appeared to be in trouble? But this was Paramus, New Jersey. When you're close to New York City, I guess you've seen it all.

When Sally came back, she was of no help either. She couldn't stop laughing. She did try to get on the PA to get some help, but she couldn't get the words out, only the laughter. She motioned to another employee to come over. Now two employees couldn't stop laughing. This was going nowhere. *I* was going nowhere. Finally, Joe passed by. You got it! After he stopped laughing, he dragged the other ladder back out to the aisle, and we took the sign down.

It was another lesson in human nature. In retail, you learn a lot about human nature. And most of the learning was very negative. Later, I would find out that I was the cause for Sally falling off the wagon. Not a toy wagon but rather the whiskey wagon. The lilac-scented gum was to cover the scent of the whiskey. As the months progressed, her ticket writing slowed down tremendously. One day, she just quit.

I felt really bad. It seems as if all the other employees knew of her problem. Soon the joke in the store was that I drove her to drink. She was a nice young lady. Since I didn't use intimidation tactics, I like to think she was afraid she was not living up to my high standards. Sure. Sure. I just needed to get the job done, but I guess it was much easier to take a drink than to do her job. I wish she would have spoken to me about her problem. The company could have assisted in getting her help. But the end result was, we were now both on our own. After a month of no help, I finally got Nancy.

Nancy had a striking face. She had dark hair with a little salt at the temples and the bluest eyes. She was a little overweight and had a one-track mind: Little Sal. I don't know why talking about sex is so prevalent in retail among the employees, but it is. But Nancy had a way of ending every discussion, work related or not, with references to Little Sal.

We'd start each day discussing what needed to get done, and she would interrupt with "Is that Little Sal talking?" She would go to lunch and bring me back a shake because she "needed to keep Little Sal fat and happy." On my birthday, she gave me two cards: one for me and, yep, one for Little Sal.

I began to get worried. She wasn't married. I wasn't married, and—you got it right—neither was Little Sal. After a while, I started putting more than an arm's length distance between us when we spoke, almost to the point of shouting. I felt like we were doing the tango. If I'd see her walking toward me, I'd talk to her while I began walking backward. If she started walking away, I'd start walking toward her still talking. We had a good rhythm going.

Yep, Nancy was unique and full of laughs. She too loved to socialize with the customers—even more so than Sally. However, she was also much slower than Sally in writing those merchandise tickets. Finally, since she did roam the store A LOT, Joe made her a cashier so she couldn't roam anymore. But when I passed her register, she would still giggle and shout out a greeting to Sal and Little Sal, and she would loudly giggle some more. Then she would apologize to the customer and begin explaining what she was giggling about as I speeded up my departure.

Many years later, I ran into Nancy at the other store in Paramus, where she was a front-end department head. She saw me first and began to giggle. I remembered that sound, and before I could spot her, I heard those long-forgotten familiar words: "How's Little Sal doin'?"

During my last season in the Paramus store, my responsibilities changed to being in charge of the storeroom and Customer Pickup. I had two full-time employees to work the storeroom and one employee to build bikes. They would unload trucks and also pull the merchandise from the storeroom when the cashier called the item back and have it waiting at the back door for the customer to pick up. Thank God there was always someone there to shout out to. I finally had a crew, a crew that actually worked. And then there was someone—probably two employees—who worked up a sweat in another way.

We sold a lot of baby products, including crib mattresses. They were usually in the racking in the storeroom, but every once in a while, one was laid out in the center of the storeroom aisle. At first, I thought nothing of it, and as I passed, I would just put it back in the rack. Then one day, Big Tom was with me passing in this area. He was my bike assembler and all-around best worker. He remarked as he put the mattress back in the rack, "I guess the mattresses are getting frisky again." I had no idea what he was talking about. Mattresses don't beget mattresses; we get them off the truck. I know 'cause I had to unload them a few times.

Then one day, as I approached the mattress area, I heard voices. I tried to sneak the rest of the way, and the closer I got, the louder the voices became. I was about to crack the case. Then I heard the side storeroom door squeak open, and it was quiet again. When I finally got to the mattresses, I again found a mattress on the floor.

Now I knew what Big Tom meant about the mattresses getting frisky. Apparently, this had been going on for years, and no one was ever caught. Well, I knew of one employee who for sure was not involved since I didn't hear that familiar giggle.

Chapter 4

The Legends, the Pioneers, the Humanity

No job in retail is easy. The long hours cause many family issues. Since I wasn't married, mine were only with my mother. Unfortunately, she wouldn't divorce me. But wives are not so tolerant or understanding, not like a mom or fellow workers also experiencing the life known as retail. Since you tended to spend more time in the store than you did at home, the store became your home. The workers became your family. There were "buds," and there were "BUDS."

In Totowa, it was quite obvious that Glen and Mary were "buds." At first, I thought they were "BUDS," but I did find out that they were only "buds" (at least from Glen's perspective). So that meant they were only "buds." But Mary's eyes came to life when she looked at Glen. She was a cute, petite, and quite-capable manager, and she always had Glen's back. Glen knew he could count on her, and he did. She covered his phone calls, supervised the work on the sales floor, did his shopping for his wife for those special occasions, and was his drinking buddy when he needed an ear to bitch to. And this was all before the age of the cell phone and the beeper.

Every merch manager needed a Mary. Mary finally got her own store, but I often wondered if it came with a "bud" or "BUD" of her own even though it is not any of my business.

There were rumors of affairs of all types. Since I was middle aging at this time, nothing was really shocking, but everything was REALLY interesting. When you know and work side by side with someone and find out (possibly) they have another side. So juicy. And I was so jealous. I barely had one side to my life. One of the most interesting stories concerned one of the DMs. She had the opportunity to invest in a well-known sneaker brand at their creation. She didn't. A WELL-KNOWN BRAND. A VERY WELL-KNOWN BRAND! I'm sure that every once in a while she still finds herself kicking herself.

Scott was not above enjoying his evenings while fixturing, but I'm told he was always bright eyed the next morning and ready to get to work while others' eyes had more of a rosy hue. I've never worked with anyone with more of a work ethic than him.

Scott immigrated to this country as a young adult. He tried pursuing a sports career in a large Midwest city bordering one of those Great Lakes. The story goes, as Scott himself liked to tell, he did have promise, but fate stepped in, and a blown knee meant a blown career. I guess the next-best thing to being a sports jock is being a retail jock. Thus, Scott began his retail career.

Most people liked Scott. Issues only arose when you didn't share his passion and enthusiasm for the company, like when you were in the store since 8:00 a.m. and at 5:30 p.m., your quitting time, Scott strolled into the store and decided he needed you to help him with a project or a new aisle layout. The last thing you would do was let him know you needed to leave the store—because you knew it would literally be the LAST THING YOU WOULD DO as an employee of the company.

Scott worked his way through the ranks quickly because of his dedication and his ability to hold the loyalty of his crew. He started his retail career as an ordinary employee who spoke broken English, became an assistant manager, quickly became a store manager, and found that he had the ability and passion for opening new stores. This is pretty handy when the company you work for is in a growth spurt.

He was a true treasure for any regional VP to possess. The northeast region won, and Scott found himself living in New Jersey. Somehow, his broken English didn't sound so broken anymore. He found a loyal band of construction companies that worked with him as he built and opened these stores, and within a matter of three years, he found himself as district manager in charge of seven or eight of the highest-volume stores in the chain. And Scott was well rewarded for his loyalty. He is one of the few self-made millionaires the company spawned.

There was no such thing as outsourcing in the good old days. The ideal situation was to have everyone on salary and just work people till they dropped or quit. When a new store was ready to be fixtured, the experienced and best employees were recruited from other stores in the market and were shipped to the new store site and put up in a local motel for the week, and the store was fixtured and stocked. At the end of a long day came an even-longer night of food and drink, and in the end, the strangest of bedfellows developed.

Reality TV at its best pales in comparison to a fixturing party with the only rewards possibly being divorce, drug addiction, and sometimes even termination.

How could you look for a job if you're working eighteen-hour days, and how could you quit without having another job to go to if you had a wife and kids to support? So most chose to stick it out, and unfortunately, marriages did end with some members of management finding consolation in the arms of "BUDS."

Chapter 5

Livingston, My Promotion, and the Punch Heard Round the Store

Finally, my own store! Well, half a store anyway. I was the ops (operations) manager. I managed the front end of the store: the money, registers, customer service, store maintenance, employee scheduling, and employee payroll. Billy put the toys on the shelves. He was the merch (merchandising) manager. Merch managers had more power than the ops managers. If the toys were not on the shelves, the registers wouldn't ring. They also received higher pay, so there was always a friendly rivalry between the two—the ops manager always wanting to second-guess the merch manager and the merch manager never wanting anything to do with the front of the store or the customers.

I was taking over for an energetic younger guy who was one training group ahead of me. I worked with him in Nanuet and in the Paramus stores. Supposedly, he did a great job and turned the Livingston store "around."

My first day at this store was a bright and sunny Monday. The merch managers were off on Monday, so it would totally be my store on my first day.

When I walked into the store, the sunny atmosphere wrapping the outside did not follow me through the entrance door. I passed the two very long rows of dull blue shopping carts as I walked through the vestibule. At the end of the vestibule, I made the sharp right that led me into the seasonal area of the store and saw the customer service area off to the left. The lighting was dull. The floors needed cleaning. The employees were walking around like they had lost their best friend. The bathrooms and break rooms were filthy. The lines of customers waiting to check out were longer than they should have been.

All in all, it was not going to be a good day.

My first day was to begin at one in the afternoon, and I would work till closing. I arrived at ten o'clock in the morning so I could get acclimated. Since I worked in this store as a trainee, some of the employees recognized me, but I recognized very few.

As I wandered the aisles (empty aisles, actually), I was thinking, *Wow, if this is considered "turned around," it won't be so bad.* And as I completed this thought, there was Billy. He hadn't changed a bit in any respect. He greeted me cordially and proceeded to explain how the weekend traffic was great, explaining the lack of merchandise in the store. He was in today since the store was receiving three trucks to help replenish the store from the weekend sales, and since Anthony's last day was on Friday, he needed to open the store.

What he really meant was that since he had to work all weekend plus come in on his day off, I would be responsible for the entire store starting at 3:00 p.m. since he did need to leave for a doctor's appointment. That was only fair, and I certainly understood his frustration. He immediately took me up front and introduced me to the head cashier. Amy would be my eyes and hands, and she would prove to be invaluable.

Amy was about twenty-three, almost a college graduate, and was looking to finish college and then go into the Manager Training Program herself. She knew the front end inside and out. Since I knew it backward and forward, we would prove to make a good team. Amy liked to run things her way until her way didn't work and there may be an issue. Then she would allow me to handle the issue her way caused. But that was fine, at least for the time being since I needed to deal with payroll and hiring and the filthiness of the store.

The store maintenance man during the day was an older gentleman named Geronimo. He was one of the Filipino contingent we were still very lucky to have working for us. He recognized me, and I was certainly happy to see he was still working at the store. He got everything done that you asked of him, but he needed to have his list. So I made sure I gave him his daily list, and he paced himself accordingly.

It seems that my idea of clean is somehow different than everyone else's idea of clean. Geronimo quickly learned what clean meant to me and did his best to achieve it. I made sure we had the cleaning supplies and equipment we needed on hand at all times, and Geronimo added his own touch. He always added orange or tangerine skins to the soapy mop water so the stores always smelled like orange blossoms.

It was actually quite nice, especially in Gigi's room (the ladies' room, as it was called). We had this little metal-house contraption that was positioned on the floor under the dividing walls of the toilet stalls. It was supposed to be the receptacle for used Kotex or tampons. Since these were the days before automatic aromatic scent dispensers, Geronimo made sure he placed the skins directly in this house on a daily basis.

He single-handedly transformed Gigi's room from an outhouse to an orange grove, and we got glowing reports from our female customers. And I have to say that the orange skins brought back memories from my childhood. We rented a railroad-style apartment, and the stove in the kitchen was gas on gas. You cooked on one side and heated the apartment with the other side. Mom used to throw orange skins on the heating side in the winter, and as they cooked, they gave off the greatest orange scent ever. And since Mom was clean to a fault, I still associate the scent of orange to clean inside and nippy outside.

Part of getting the store clean included some merchandising changes required for season, which was fast approaching. This meant that hiring for seasonal help was also happening. Seasonal help back then was like normal help today: no real work ethic unless constantly supervised. They are tired. They come from their daytime job, their bread and butter, and expect to hang till closing to make some extra cash for the holidays. Since my main responsibility was the front of the store, this included the hiring requirements.

Livingston, New Jersey, then was an exclusive community for the most part with children of privilege. So hiring was difficult. One cannot be mean, nasty, or crack the whip, 'cause those you were lucky enough to hire would walk.

I'm basically a nice guy. I also am a good judge of people. I tried to only hire people who would be good workers. But you know, bottom line, we had to be hired up, or else the work would not get done at all.

But I really didn't have deadbeats in the store. Some were just slower than others. One of these guys worked in the storeroom and at customer pickup. I think his name was Allen. A super nice guy. Respectful and humble. He didn't socialize. He just did his work.

Well, we also needed to staff up management and I was given an assistant manager from our Paramus store.

Now, in Paramus, there were no hiring issues. It was on a major highway. It was on a bus route to all the local towns along that route. So you could push and shove and militarize your employees, and if they left, you just hired someone else to replace them. This was the mentality Matt brought to our store.

Matt was on the same schedule as me. He walked the floor and took care of the customer pickup area. At around 12:30 a.m., I was in the tower at the front of the store closing out the cash. I could see our employees scurrying around the sales floor trying to put it back in order so they could go home. It was very quiet 'cause everyone wanted to do their re-shop and leave. And because it was so quiet, we all heard the proverbial pin drop. But it was a fist hitting a face. It happened at the back of the store, but it sounded like it happened right in front of me.

It appears that Matt was using tactics from Paramus and pushing Allen to do more than anyone could or should be expected to do since he, Allen, was quiet and reserved and not likely to argue the point. And he didn't argue; he just punched Matt in the face and walked out, never to be seen again. Matt couldn't file a complaint since other employees heard him taunting Allen. He did try to intimidate other associates during his tenure in our store, but they all put Matt in his place. I guess Allen did also, in his own way.

Matt soon decided that retail wasn't for him and left to be a teacher. Well, working in a store is similar to monitoring children. I don't think Matt saw the similarity. I can clearly visualize those kids putting him in his place.

Chapter 6

I'll Take Manhattan, the Bronx, and Staten Island Too! Ooh, and Brooklyn

Overall, we did well that Christmas season in Livingston. And to my surprise, I was summoned to the area office, where I was offered the position of human resource manager recently vacated. I was manager number 3, and the duties and responsibilities included recruiting store managers for the New York area, which included Brooklyn, Staten Island, and Long Island.

The New York metro area encompassed perhaps thirty square miles, but what different worlds these three boroughs were from each other. The Long Island staff was respectful, courteous, and professional when dealing with customers. Brooklyn staff gave back to customers what they received from customers, and this included cursing and blows when necessary. After the shock wore off, I learned that this was the standard operating procedure for Brooklyn—no one got over on anyone in Brooklyn. Staten Island was a mixture of the two. It was an experience conducting harassment seminars with the Brooklyn teams, but no group of people knew how to have more fun. After all, work, in the end, needs to be fun.

One of my official duties as HR rep for New York was working with the district manager to plan the end-of-sales-year celebration. Trying to find a central location in the metro area was not as simple as one might think. We looked at several venues in the West Orange area.

One of the sites was actually where the pool scene in *Cocoon* was filmed. During the course of the search, my car decided to act up. But since the DM drives all the time, she relished being driven whenever possible. My words *car trouble* seemed to go in one ear and out the other.

One day, she had a few hours free and wanted to check out a location in the Flushing Meadow, New York, area (the site of the 1964 New York World's Fair). So in my car we go through the Lincoln Tunnel on our way to the Midtown Tunnel. We hit lots of traffic on West Thirty-Fourth Street. My car tended to act up when idling too long, so the traffic was not a good thing.

Finally, we get into the Midtown Tunnel, and as we began to go round a bend in the tunnel, my car shut off, leaving me with no steering and no brakes. I threw it into neutral and began turning the ignition. *Groan, groan, groan, vroom.* Thank God *vroom* came right as we straightened from the curve and as traffic was slowing down again. The DM's high hair was a little lower, and she promised to listen should there be a next time I'd say I was having car trouble. She patted me on the back and thanked the angel I had on my shoulder, for it had to be divine intervention that kept us and those around us safe. By the way, she was also the DM who could have made a fortune in the sneaker industry.

The event did not take place in Flushing Meadow but at a catering hall in West Orange, New Jersey. It was a great success. I did well. So when restructuring happened at the area office that spring, I was saved and given a position in Inventory Control as an assistant inventory control manager.

As is the norm in retail, nothing stays the same for very long. As an inventory control manager, I was given my own categories of toys to balance. No profits could be made if the merchandise was in the warehouse and not in the stores and on the shelves. I had to ensure that no merchandise under my care stayed in the warehouse. We did weekly reports that indicated where the stock was at that point in time. Shipments were made to stores based on volume of sales.

All stores needed a full week's supply at all times. Sounds simple, but actually, it could become complicated. We also did store-to-store transfers, interarea transfers, and the search for items that a store had assigned to it but could not find since they were showing no sales for a long period. The latter was the hardest to accomplish since it was last on the priority list of our office clerks to place into the system since they were really just odds and ends of items, but it was still a priority for the company to ensure ALL merchandise was on the sales floor. My manager did take this report seriously since a small part of his year-end bonus was based on this report being minimal.

My first priority were my hot items. The balancing needed to be done by Tuesday at the latest so they could be keypunched into the systems and loaded on the next trucks going to the stores and be in the stores for the weekend.

Oh yeah, I forgot to tell you about my other major responsibility: I composed the weekly black-and-white newspaper ads for our market. These ads needed to be completed by Thursday and overnighted to the area newspapers. These had to arrive on Friday so they could be included in the Sunday editions. The items in these ads were suggested by the corporate advertising office based on the buyer recommendations.

I received enough copies of the week's ad for the number of newspapers involved. They also gave me alternate items in case some of my stores didn't have the items being suggested by the buyers. All the stores in a newspaper's reach needed to have all items advertised. So all items needed to be punched up in the system to ensure their availability at the store on that Sunday. If an alternate needed to be used, then it needed to be pasted over the questionable item with rubber cement. Yes, these were the days before sophisticated computer systems—the good old days. But it was the era of the black-and-white ROP ad.

Once the ads were set, the stores needed to be advised of the items so they could ensure these items were on the sales floor en masse prior to the ads breaking. Bottom line: I was a very busy man. I didn't have time to work those "not on floor item" reports. That meant I needed to take these huge green-bar-paper reports home for the weekend. Rain or shine, hot or cold, these reports needed to be worked every week.

It was a great conversation starter at the beach. Most people lugged a cooler; I lugged a ten-pound green-bar-paper report. On a good weekend, I gave instructions to friends, and instead of games or drinking, there were four or five of us indicating transfers on this report.

The clerk in charge of entering these transfers in the system also felt like she had a day at the beach as she brushed away the sand trapped in the pages. Since she didn't smile that much, I loved glancing in her direction when she was working this report to see the corners of her mouth rise. She was a dedicated and conscientious employee and certainly overworked. I'm glad that I could make her smile on these days. She did tell me once that just because I was overworked didn't mean that *she* had to be overworked too, and then she laughed. I'm glad she appreciated me.

The area offices were part of the regional warehouse. And since ours was only thirty miles from corporate headquarters, the corporate advertising department personnel were very friendly with us, and we developed a certain rapport with them. Also, corporate offices were staffed in large part from people from the area offices. My manager had recommended several of his people for corporate positions in the past. One Monday, I walked into his office for my weekly meeting, and he told me to take a ride to corporate. I had to be there for an eleven o'clock appointment with the director of corporate promotions.

It took five years of long hours, hard work, missed family functions, and many relationships built with customers, fellow employees, managers, directors, even company vice presidents, but before I knew it, I was a corporate citizen once again. I would be replacing the current corporate promotions manager who was going back to Detroit to be closer to family. He would still be part of the company, but at the store level. He did a great job but couldn't get used to the New York–New Jersey metro area. So after two years, he and his wife decided to return home, allowing me to become part of the corporate toy box.

It would prove to be another type of toy box, but a toy box nonetheless. And as with any toy box, it was filled with many years of uncertainty, adventure, exploration, learning, and a whole lot of fun.

Sal Panicci was born into a lower-middle-class family in the 1950s in Paterson, New Jersey, the same town as Lou Costello. In fact, his dad grew up in the same neighborhood as Lou and knew him well. Until the age of ten, he thought all families were like his. He played and grew up in a neighborhood where most families had two parents. The fathers always worked, and sometimes, so did the mothers.

In the Panicci household, Dad went to work even when he was sick, and Mom stayed home to tend to the apartment and the three kids. But unlike the other families in the neighborhood whose dads were paying off homes and cars with their salaries, Papa Al usually deposited his pay at the local gin mill or with the local bookie.

On a rainy winter afternoon in Sal's tenth year, his dad finally came home to find his few bags of belongings on the back porch, and Tina, Sal's mom, found she had the fortitude to be a single parent before it was fashionable, the norm, or politically acceptable.

Sal went to the local public grammar school, PS#5, then on to the local private high school, which Mom could not afford. But somehow, he graduated from Don Bosco Technical High School as valedictorian with a 4.0 GPA and went on to Seton Hall University, where he graduated suma cum laude.

Sal and his two siblings grew up under financially tough circumstances, so higher education was not in his thoughts. But thanks to Father Paul Grauls, his high school guidance counselor, Sal had a full scholarship to Seton Hall University.

After graduating from college, Sal became a productive corporate citizen. His first job was as a TV cameraman at Prudential Insurance Company in Newark, New Jersey. This was on a project basis. When the projects were completed for the fiscal year, he became an advertising manager for various industrial products manufacturers. But he found himself being laid off every two to three years.

Then a friend told him to try retail. "Retailers never lay off," this friend advised.

Well, more than thirty years later, Sal proved his friend wrong. Retailers *do* lay off associates. Sometimes even for bogus reasons.

However, the first years at Toys"R"Us were a true learning experience and set the foundation for many years of success at Toys"R"Us corporate. The main lessons learned were that no matter what the position,

- there is never enough time to complete a project;
- there are always too many projects to juggle;
- there are always too many hands stirring the pot but never enough to actually do the work;
- there will always be revisions at the point when it is normally impossible to accomplish project changes;
- there will always be heated discussions with all persons needed to accomplish these revisions, including outside sources; and
- regardless of the success or lack of success of the project, the end result needs to be upper management's desired goal.

Yet despite all the challenges, it was fun. Certainly, every day was a lesson in humanity, humility, and compromise. It was life! We had all ethnicities, genders, and religions in all positions—whether of great importance or not so important. In reality, we all did our jobs, and we all celebrated everyone's success with no one telling us we had to or how to. We all shared in success, and we all shared in failure. It was life. At least, this is the way I care to remember. Looking forward to sharing some remembrances of TRU corporate with you.

www.ingramcontent.com/pod-product-compliance
Lightning Source LLC
Chambersburg PA
CBHW031003180726
47993CB00018B/1545